Look to Your Stars

A selection of thoughts for
each sign of the Zodiac

———

Edited by Louise Bachelder

Illustrated by Stanley Clough

PETER PAUPER PRESS
Mount Vernon, New York

Is It Written in the Stars?

"The contemplation of celestial things," states Cicero, "will make a man both speak and think more sublimely and magnificently when he descends to human affairs."

"It is the stars—the stars above us, that govern our condition," writes Shakespeare, while on the other hand Jeremy Taylor maintains, "A wise man shall overrule his stars and have a greater influence upon his own content than all the constellations and planets of the firmament."

It is left to the pleasure of the reader to determine to what measure he agrees with Cicero, Shakespeare, or Jeremy Taylor and to how great an extent he is influenced by his particular sign.

It will be noted that the dates of the signs of the Zodiac are not absolute and may differ from the reader's source of reference.

The quotations in this little book are grouped according to the characteristics of each of the twelve signs of the Zodiac, with a considered disregard for the "stars" under which the authors themselves came into the world. We invite each of our readers to turn to his own sign to peruse the selected quotations, and then go on to enjoy the others!

THE EDITOR

ARIES
March 21-April 19

Aries, a Fire Sign symbolizing zeal, courage, and enthusiasm, is the first of the twelve signs, arriving in the Spring of the year when all nature comes to life. The pioneering instinct is strong in one born at this time. He has great ambitions, is a leader, and a "go-getter." Action is the key word! Challenge gives an opportunity to prove superiority. His efforts are devoted to useful ends as a reformer and champion of the weak. His Symbol is the Ram.

Sometimes an Arien overestimates his own abilities and fails to see the other person's point of view. Proud and resentful of criticism, he then realizes that to get things done he may have to do them himself. His mind is quick and he can with expediency deal with a situation diplomatically.

There is nothing more satisfying to an Arien than to dash off on a trip where he finds it easy to strike up new acquaintances. He is at the same time a home lover, an excellent host with friends welcome at all times.

Ariens make good doctors, dentists, and engineers. Under this sign too are many pioneers in the world of music and motion pictures.

―――――――

CONQUERING, holding, daring, venturing
    as we go the unknown ways,
Pioneers! O pioneers!

WALT WHITMAN

THE method of the enterprising is to plan with audacity and execute with vigor; to sketch out a map of possibilities, and then to treat them as probabilities.

CHRISTIAN N. BOVÉE

THE fact is that to do anything in this world worth doing, we must not stand back shivering and thinking of the cold and danger, but jump in and scramble through as well as we can.

SYDNEY SMITH

Let us do or die.

JOHN FLETCHER

THE use of travelling is to regulate imagination by reality, and instead of thinking how things may be, to see them as they are.

SAMUEL JOHNSON

THE right of commanding is no longer an advantage transmitted by nature; like an inheritance, it is the fruit of labors, the price of courage.

VOLTAIRE

TEN people will give you a dinner, for one who will offer you a bed and a breakast.

GEORGE MACDONALD

How much a dunce that has been sent
   to roam
Excels a dunce that has been kept at
   home!

WILLIAM COWPER

SOME bold adventurers disdain
The limits of their little reign,
And unknown regions dare descry.

THOMAS GRAY

PLEASANTEST
Of all ties is the tie of host and guest.

AESCHYLUS

EXPEDIENCY is a law of nature. The camel is a wonderful animal, but the desert made the camel.

BENJAMIN DISRAELI

PRIDE is at the bottom of all great mistakes.

JOHN RUSKIN

HE that has energy enough in his constitution to root out a vice should go a little further, and try to plant a virtue in its place; otherwise he will have his labor to renew. A strong soil that has produced weeds may be made to produce wheat with far less difficulty than it would cost to make it produce nothing.

CHARLES CALEB COLTON

THERE are pioneer souls that blaze
   their paths
   Where highways never ran.

SAM WALTER FOSS

SOMETHING attempted, something done,
Has earned a night's repose.

HENRY WADSWORTH LONGFELLOW

ADVENTURES are to the adventurous.

BENJAMIN DISRAELI

ONE of the pleasantest things in the world is going on a journey; but I like to go by myself. . . . The soul of a journey is liberty to think, feel, do just as one pleases.

WILLIAM HAZLITT

TAURUS
April 20 - May 20

*T*here is no sign that has the practical *"stick-to-it-iveness"* of Taurus, an Earth-Sign, the most determined of all those of the Zodiac. A Taurean, symbolized by the Bull, has both feet on the ground, knows where he is going, and will push aside obstacles and wear down opposition with a steady and relentless striving. Once pro-

voked, he can display temper and be stubborn to a fault, though generally he is amiable, affectionate, and loyal to family and friends.

Taurus is the money sign, and the Taurean is likely to worship money, the things it can buy, and the security it can give. A lover of possessions, he fills a basic need by acquiring the good things of life. Happily with his understanding of how money should be handled and with his attention to detail, he not only makes sound his own affairs but helps others less fortunate than himself.

Business-like Taurus with his practical ability also has artistic talents, and creative expression is essential to his temperament. Bankers and business men in this sign are often successful in the fields of art, music, and decorating.

Ruled by Venus, the planet of charm and magnetism, the Taurus individual instinctively attracts people to him.

DILIGENCE is the mother of good fortune.
MIGUEL DE CERVANTES

THOU, O Venus, art sole mistress of the nature of things, and without thee nothing rises up into the divine realms of life, nothing grows to be lovely or glad.

LUCRETIUS

THE heights by great men reached and
    kept
  Were not attained by sudden flight,
But they while their companions slept
  Were toiling upward in the night.

HENRY WADSWORTH LONGFELLOW

I AM in earnest. l will not equivocate; I will not excuse; I will not retreat a single inch; and I will be heard!

WILLIAM LLOYD GARRISON

PROVIDENCE requires three things of us before it will help us — a stout heart, a strong arm, and a stiff upper lip.

THOMAS CHANDLER HALIBURTON

To endure is the first thing a child ought to learn, and that which he will have most need to know.

JEAN JACQUES ROUSSEAU

ALL men are in some degree impressed by the face of the world; some men even to delight. This love of beauty is taste. Others have the same love in such success that, not content with admiring, they seek to embody it in new forms. The creation of beauty is art.

RALPH WALDO EMERSON

RICHES well got, and well used, are a great blessing.

PROVERB

VENUS, thy eternal sway
All the race of men obey.

EURIPIDES

BUT certain winds will make men's temper bad.

GEORGE ELIOT

READY money is Aladdin's lamp.

LORD BYRON

WHATSOEVER thy hand findeth to do, do it with thy might.

ECCLES. 9:10

MONEY, which represents the prose of life, and which is hardly spoken of in parlors without an apology, is, in its effects and laws, as beautiful as roses.

RALPH WALDO EMERSON

CHARM is of use in all things and pleases everybody.

COMTESSE DIANE DE POITIERS

BEAUTY lies in the harmony between man and his industry. Beauty is expression.

JEAN MILLET

OBSTINACY is the sister of constancy.

MICHEL DE MONTAIGNE

DEEDS, not words.

JOHN FLETCHER

THERE is nothing more to be esteemed than a manly firmness and decision of character. I like a person who knows his own mind and sticks to it; who sees at once what, in given circumstances, is to be done, and does it.

WILLIAM HAZLITT

GEMINI
May 21 - June 21

*Gemini, a dynamo of intellectual energy,
with an unlimited range of ideas, is restless and does not like to feel held down.
His live, facile mind and roving feet want
to be free. Happiest when surrounded by
people, he is a perceptive individual with
a tremendous awareness of everything
and everyone about him. Blessed with a*

15

subtle sense of humor, a light touch, and a winning personality, the Geminian attracts and keeps many friends, often becoming a "father confessor" to those in trouble.

Ingenious and imaginative, he tends to become over-involved. With varied interests, he must have a creative outlet to develop himself to the full, but his intense drive may over-expend his physical stamina. He needs to learn to concentrate if he is to utilize his talents. Due to the dual nature of his being, symbolized by the Twins, he may feel contradictory desires and tensions. It is important that he try to govern himself intellectually rather than emotionally.

The sign of Gemini is ruled by Mercury, the planet of quicksilver. Events happen rapidly in the life of Gemini. With his Mercurial gifts, he often understands things more quickly than do others and is apt to become impatient.

An artist in communication and a fluent talker, Gemini often succeeds in the fields of journalism, publishing, teaching, or selling. His is the most adaptable of all the signs. His Element is Air which symbolizes intellect and the ability to move with ease among people.

IMPULSE is, after all, the best linguist; its logic, if not conformable, to Aristotle, cannot fail to be most convincing.

HENRY DAVID THOREAU

IMAGINATION disposes of everything; it creates beauty, justice, and happiness, which is everything in this world.

BLAISE PASCAL

CURIOSITY is one of the permanent and certain characteristics of a vigorous intellect.

SAMUEL JOHNSON

OCCUPATION is the necessary basis of all enjoyment.

LEIGH HUNT

RESTLESS at home and ever prone to range.

JOHN DRYDEN

17

BLESSED are they who have the gift of making friends, for it is one of God's best gifts. It involves many things, but above all, the power of going out of one's self, and appreciating whatever is noble and loving in another.

THOMAS HUGHES

THE man who seeks but one thing in life,
    and but one,
May hope to achieve it before life is done;
But he who seeks all things, wherever he
    goes
Only reaps from the hopes which around
    him he sows
    A harvest of barren regrets.

GEORGE MEREDITH

OTHER relaxations are peculiar to certain times, places and stages of life, but the study of letters is the nourishment of our youth, and the joy of our old age. They throw an additional splendor on prosperity, and are the resource and consolation of adversity; they delight at home, and are no embarrassment abroad.

CICERO

THE greatness of an artist or a writer does not depend on what he has in common with other artists and writers, but on what he has peculiar to himself.

ALEXANDER SMITH

WITH thee conversing, I forget all times,
   All seasons, and their change.

JOHN MILTON

WE have been born to associate with our fellow-men, and to join in community with the human race.

CICERO

JOY is a flame which association alone can keep alive, and which goes out unless communicated.

ALPHONSE LAMARTINE

THERE are some men and women in whose company we are always at our best. All the best stops in our nature are drawn out, and we find a music in our souls never felt before.

WILLIAM HENRY DRUMMOND

CANCER
June 22 - July 22

Cancer, whose Element is Water, which symbolizes emotion and psychic power, can be the most domestic of all the signs.

He is home-loving, fond of family, and social life. He likes good food and enjoys cooking. Sensitive, deceptively timid, feeling a great need to be loved, Cancer wants

20

security and seeks it in devious ways. The Crab, the symbol of this sign, clutches tightly what he wants in his claw, defying even death without letting go. So Cancer uses much the same method in holding on to people, money, and possessions. Children of Cancer parents may become victims of over-devotion.

Because of this passion or holding onto things, Cancer enjoys collecting. Glassware, the crystallized form of his element water, is a favorite, as is silver, the color ruled by the Moon. He likes to collect sentimental pieces pertaining to the family and cannot throw anything away. He loves the past. He is strongly patriotic in his love for his country.

Cancer is emotional and reacts more through his feelings than through his mind. He is deeply intuitive. He may be inclined to be moody and dramatize the small things which upset him and make him nervous.

Any work that helps others is right for Cancer. A homemaking skill carried out on a large scale may prove a profitable career. Teaching could be a successful field. The sea is attractive to him and work pertaining to liquids is ideal. Arts which offer free play for his imagination and emotions can be an absorbing and creative outlet.

———————

To be happy at home is the ultimate result of all ambition, the end to which every enterprise and labor tends, and of which every desire prompts the prosecution.

SAMUEL JOHNSON

COOKERY is become an art, a noble science. . . .

ROBERT BURTON

HE is the happiest, be he king or peasant, who finds peace in his home.

JOHANN WOLFGANG VON GOETHE

No possessions are good, but by the good use we make of them; without which wealth, power, friends, and servants, do but help to make our lives more unhappy.

SIR WILLIAM TEMPLE

WHERE is the man who owes nothing to the land in which he lives? Whatever the land may be, he owes to it the most precious thing possessed by man, the morality of his actions and the love of virtue.

JEAN-JACQUES ROUSSEAU

IN many ways doth the full heart reveal
The presence of the love it would conceal.

SAMUEL TAYLOR COLERIDGE

To spoil children is to deceive them concerning life; life herself does not spoil us.

COMTESSE DIANE DE POITIERS

I LOVE the sea as I do my own soul.

HEINRICH HEINE

THE illusion that times that were are better than those that are, has probably pervaded all ages.

HORACE GREELEY

A COMFORTABLE house is a great source of happiness. It ranks immediately after health and a good conscience.

SYDNEY SMITH

LEO
July 23 - August 22

Leo, the Lion, is the sign of exuberance, a Fire Sign, denoting a strong personality, and an ability to please an audience. Things which suggest power are attractive to him because Leo is ruled by the Sun. Leo is a leader of great personal magnetism bestowed on him by his Sun sign.

An extrovert, he shines on all, but is apt

to roar like a lion, the symbol of his sign, if things do not go his way. Others may feel, and rightly so, that their points of view are not of interest to him. Despite the fact that Leo is an "I" centered person, imperious and self-assured, people are drawn to him because of his warmth and generosity of spirit.

Leo rules the heart. Love and romanticism are essential to him though he often neglects others in his devotion to the one he loves.

Leo has a trusting nature. Frank and direct, he likes to exaggerate and sets himself royally above others. He cannot bear to fail and takes pride in all he does.

He has an artistic and creative imagination, and he may express this in a setting of beauty and splendor in a lovely home.

Leo works best when he has sole authority in an executive position. In the theatre he may find a career to satisfy his sense of the dramatic. Politics is another field in which he can find an outlet for his self-confidence and zest for life.

To do anything, to dig a hole in the ground, to plant a cabbage, to hit a mark, to move a shuttle, to work a pattern — in a word, to attempt to produce any effect, and to succeed, has something in it that gratifies the lover of power.

WILLIAM HAZLITT

The lion is (beyond dispute)
Allow'd the most majestic brute;
His valor and his gen'rous mind
Prove him superior of his kind.

JOHN GAY

Let not thy will roar when thy power can but whisper.

THOMAS FULLER

Rather than be less,
Car'd not to be at all.

JOHN MILTON

Were I to choose a religion, I would probably become a worshipper of the sun. It gives life and fertility to all things. It is the true God of the earth.

NAPOLEON I

ENTHUSIASM is the genius of sincerity, and truth accomplishes no victories without it. . . . The man who is capable of generating enthusiasm can't be whipped.

EDWARD ROBERT BULWER-LYTTON

THERE is a vast deal of vital air in loving words.

WALTER SAVAGE LANDOR

THE night has a thousand eyes,
    And the day but one,
Yet the light of the bright world dies
    With the dying sun.

FRANCIS WILLIAM BOURDILLON

EGOISM is the very essence of a noble soul.

FRIEDRICH WILHELM NIETZSCHE

ROMANCE is always young.

JOHN GREENLEAF WHITTIER

I AM certain of nothing but of the holiness of the heart's affections and the truth of Imagination. What the Imagination seizes as Beauty must be Truth.

JOHN KEATS

VIRGO
August 23 - September 22

Virgo, an Earth Sign, capable and industrious, with a remarkable memory, likes to help people and is committed to worthy causes. This is the sign of service and Virgo's greatest happiness comes through doing for others. He has an involvement with life, and a Virgo does not realize his

28

own potential unless he can fulfill his nature in this way.

Virgo is a down-to-earth person with a practical mentality. His intelligence rules his emotions. A perfectionist, he analyzes, dissects, and studies before coming to any conclusion. He is overly concerned with matters of diet and health. His attention to minute details and his discriminating taste can at times make him an irritating critic of friends and family.

He does everything in a scientific way, thinking along lines of known facts. Virgo does not concern himself with the mysteries of life. He likes to work alone and does not seek the limelight. He is modest, is apt to underestimate his own importance, and is usually blessed with a good sense of humor. Influenced by his Earth Sign, he prefers the simple life and is democratic in his relationships.

Virgo is interested in the reasons behind the actions of others and makes a good critic. He is also happy in personnel work, in medicine, in research and in statistics.

THE superior man is distressed by the limitations of his ability; he is not distressed by the fact that men do not recognize the ability that he has.

CONFUCIUS

HE was in logic a great critic,
Profoundly skill'd in analytic;
He could distinguish and divide
A hair 'twixt south and south-west side.

SAMUEL BUTLER

ALL weighty things are done in solitude, that is, without society. The means of improvement consist not in projects, or in any violent designs, for these cool, and cool very soon, but in patient practicing for whole long days, by which I make the thing clear to my highest reason.

JEAN PAUL RICHTER

PERFECTION does not exist. To understand it is the triumph of human intelligence; to desire to possess it is the most dangerous kind of madness.

ALFRED DE MUSSET

To talk in public, to think in solitude, to read and to hear, to inquire and answer inquiries, is the business of a scholar.

SAMUEL JOHNSON

THE work of science is to substitute facts for appearances, and demonstrations for impressions.

JOHN RUSKIN

THE desire of perfection is the worst disease that ever afflicted the human mind.

LOUIS FONTANES

HELL itself must yield to industry.

BEN JONSON

THE mark of the man of the world is absence of pretension. He does not make a speech; he takes a low business tone, avoids all brag, is nobody, dresses plainly, promises not at all, performs much, speaks in monosyllables, hugs his fact. He calls his employment by its lowest name, and so takes from evil tongues their sharpest weapon.

RALPH WALDO EMERSON

TRUE humanity consists not in a squeamish ear; it consists not in starting or shrinking at tales of misery, but in a disposition of heart to relieve it. True humanity appertains rather to the mind than to the nerves, and prompts men to use real and active endeavors to execute the actions which it suggests.

CHARLES JAMES FOX

BETTER to take pleasure in a rose than to put its root under a microscope.

OSCAR WILDE

IT is not work that kills men; it is worry. Work is healthy: you can hardly put more upon a man than he can bear. Worry is rust upon the blade.

HENRY WARD BEECHER

THE habit of analysis has a tendency to wear away the feelings.

JOHN STUART MILL

THIS world is a comedy to those who think, a tragedy to those who feel.

HORACE WALPOLE

LIBRA
September 23 - October 22

*T*he symbol of the sign of Libra is the
Scales of Justice. The one born under this
sign balances everything and respects justice and honor. He is ready to write letters
to representatives, to go to war, to do anything and everything to restore balance.
Equilibrium is important to him. A peace-

maker, he is disturbed to witness injustice and unfairness.

Libra makes an ideal parent as he is reasonable and willing to listen to the other side of the story. This tendency to see both sides of a situation can be a negative quality when Libra fails to act because he cannot make a decision.

Venus-ruled, Libra is gentle, charming, affectionate, and diplomatic. Family life is important to him, and he makes a most desirable marriage partner. Because he thinks first of the other person, he is popular and has a talent for getting along with people. He is understanding and sympathetic.

A Libran is precise and fastidious. In his effort to please he is apt to be over-zealous in his desire for perfection. Lacking spontaneity, he plans and re-plans and is extremely "time-conscious."

Born under the symbol of the Scales, he is cooperative and likes to share. He makes a good partner in a business undertaking, and his creative ability is strong in the field of arts. A Libran has the ingenuity and cleverness to make a thing of beauty from cast-off materials or objects. His well-balanced temperament makes him a good critic. An Air Sign, Libra has high intellect and is philosophically inclined.

ASSIST him who is carrying his burden, but by no means him who is laying it aside.

SENECA

WE get back our mete as we measure,
We cannot do wrong and feel right,
Nor can we give pain and feel pleasure,
For justice avenges each slight.

ALICE CARY

THE two powers which in my opinion constitute a wise man are those of bearing and forbearing.

EPICTETUS

THE nearer you come into relation with a person, the more necessary do tact and courtesy become.

OLIVER WENDELL HOLMES

SYMPATHY is a thing to be encouraged apart from humane consideration, because it supplies us with the materials for wisdom.

ROBERT LOUIS STEVENSON

AN honest man nearly always thinks justly.

JEAN JACQUES ROUSSEAU

BLESSED are the peacemakers, for they shall be called the children of God.

MATTHEW 5:9

'TIS death to me to be at enmity; I hate it, and desire all men's love.

WILLIAM SHAKESPEARE

KINDNESS is the principal of tact, and respect for others the first condition of *savoir-vivre*.

HENRI-FRÉDÉRIC AMIEL

WE are born for cooperation, as are the feet, the hands, the eyelids and the upper and lower jaws.

MARCUS AURELIUS

THE secret of success in society is a certain heartiness and sympathy.

RALPH WALDO EMERSON

WHO will not mercy unto others show, how can he mercy ever hope to have?

HERBERT SPENCER

Do as you would be done by is the surest method of pleasing.

LORD CHESTERFIED

HE who considers too much will perform little.

JOHANN FRIEDRICH VON SCHILLER

IT is because of justice that man is a god to man and not a wolf.

FRANCIS BACON

KINDNESS in ourselves is the honey that blunts the sting of unkindness in another.

WALTER SAVAGE LANDOR

To make a man pleased with himself, let me tell you, is doing a very great thing.

SAMUEL JOHNSON

SCORPIO
October 23 - November 21

This sign, called at times "the home of the harnessed Mars," describes the determination, the strength, and the concentration that are characteristic of those born under Scorpio, whose energy is intense and whose purpose is invincible. Each individual knows what he wants and goes after it fearlessly with the courage of his con-

victions, sticking to them, martyr-like, though sometimes doing himself injury. Thus doth the scorpion, the symbol of this sign, who will sting himself to death when surrounded by a ring of fire.

Scorpio is a loyal friend to those he has decided to accept,—helpful, tender, and sympathetic when real problems present themselves. Direct and without sentimentality, he is generous with understanding and practical help. With his shrewd mind Scorpio likes to maneuver situations and people and inclines to be possessive. Secretive about himself, he draws others out with his intuitive power, which is strong under this sign. He is able to sense what people are thinking, and this gives him an unusual advantage.

With this gift of perception, Scorpio, a Water Sign, makes an excellent detective, doctor, or psychiatrist. Scorpio is also concerned with money; many high financiers come under this sign.

ENERGY is eternal delight.

WILLIAM BLAKE

WE care not how many see us in choler, when we rave and bluster, and make as much noise and bustle as we can; but if the kindest and most generous affection comes across us, we suppress every sign of it, and hide ourselves in nooks and covert.

WALTER SAVAGE LANDOR

THE power of perception is that which we call the understanding.

JOHN LOCKE

IT is always a poor way of reading the hearts of others to try to conceal our own.

WILLIAM HAZLITT

LET come what will, I mean to bear it out,
And either live with glorious victory
Or die with fame, renowned in chivalry:
He is not worthy of the honeycomb
That shuns the hive because the bees have
    stings.

WILLIAM SHAKESPEARE

THAT cause is strong which has, not a multitude, but one strong man behind it.

JAMES RUSSELL LOWELL

I'LL speak to it, though hell itself should gape, and bid me hold my peace.

WILLIAM SHAKESPEARE

PEOPLE addicted to secrecy are so without knowing why; they are not so for cause, but for secrecy's sake.

WILLIAM HAZLITT

WHEN moral courage feels that it is in the right, there is no personal daring of which it is incapable.

LEIGH HUNT

IF we command our wealth, we shall be rich and free; if our wealth commands us, we are poor indeed.

EDMUND BURKE

MEN are seldom more innocently employed than when they are honestly making money.

SAMUEL JOHNSON

NOTHING is so strong as gentleness; nothing so gentle as real strength.

ST. FRANCIS DE SALES

CONCENTRATION is the secret of strength in politics, in war, in trade, in short in all management of human affairs.

RALPH WALDO EMERSON

HE who reigns within himself, and rules passions, desires, and fears is more than a king.

JOHN MILTON

WE must be afraid of neither poverty nor exile nor imprisonment; of fear itself only should we be afraid.

EPICTETUS

THE power of a man is his present means to obtain some future apparent good.

THOMAS HOBBES

NOTHING relieves and ventilates the mind like a resolution.

JOHN BURROUGHS

ENERGY will do anything that can be done in this world; and no talents, no circumstances, no opportunities, will make a two-legged animal a man without it.

JOHN WOLFGANG VON GOETHE

SAGITTARIUS
November 22 - December 21

Sagittarius is known for his physical and mental activity. His symbol, the Archer, denotes his interest in the field of sports. Open air, sunshine, and exercise are essential for his well-being, and travel also is most beneficial. Sagittarius is forceful in speech and is the most philosophical of all the signs. He is exceedingly independent

43

and his powers of reason are strong. Influenced by luck-giving Jupiter, he is optimistic and good-natured, democratic and honest, friendly and affectionate. His enthusiasm is contagious, and he joins in enterprises to help others.

A Fire Sign, he is often quick to wrath, which can make difficult a domestic situation. However, his anger is of short duration.

Sagittarius has so many interests that he is not dependent on family life. Often he leaves the parental nest at an early age and does not hasten to marry. He needs freedom in any relationship. Sagittarius is sometimes referred to as the bachelor sign.

In health he is fortunate; there are more octogenarians born under this sign than under any other. He keeps his alert mental powers until the end.

Sagittarius does best in a field where he may operate as his own boss. He has little patience with being supervised or with red tape. The fields of law, publishing, active ministry, travelling, or philosophy attract many in this sign. His enthusiasm and impulsiveness make him a good salesman or advertising executive. His range of interests is wide but in each he is sincere.

IT is exercise alone that supports the spirits, and keeps the mind in vigor.

CICERO

FREEDOM all solace to man gives;
He lives at ease, that freely lives.

JOHN BARBOUR

WONDROUS is the strength of cheerfulness, altogether past calculation its powers of endurance.

THOMAS CARLYLE

I WAS not born to be forced. I will breathe after my own fashion. . . . If a plant cannot live according to its nature, it dies; and so a man.

HENRY DAVID THOREAU

DEMOCRACY means not "I am as good as you are, but "You are as good as I am."

THEODORE PARKER

THERE are many troubles which you cannot cure by the Bible and the hymn-book, but which you can cure by a good perspiration and a breath of fresh air.

HENRY WARD BEECHER

WHENEVER you are angry, be assured that it is not only a present evil, but you have increased a habit.

EPICTETUS

To know how to grow old is the master-work of wisdom and one of the most difficult chapters in the great art of living.

HENRI-FRÉDÉRIC AMIEL

PHILOSOPHY alone makes the mind invincible, and places us out of the reach of fortune, so that all her arrows fall short of us.

. . . . .

Philosophy is the art and law of life, and it teaches us what to do in all cases, and like good marksmen, to hit the white at any distance.

SENECA

MANY blessings do the advancing years bring with them.

HORACE

THE first step toward greatness is to be honest, says the proverb; but the proverb fails to state the case strong enough. Honesty is not only "the first step toward greatness,"—it is greatness itself.

CHRISTIAN N. BOVÉE

CONFIDENCE in others' honesty is no light testimony of one's own integrity.

MICHEL DE MONTAIGNE

I TRAVEL not to go anywhere, but to go.

ROBERT LOUIS STEVENSON

NOTHING great was ever achieved without enthusiasm.

RALPH WALDO EMERSON

WHAT reason would grope for in vain, spontaneous impulse ofttimes achieves at a stroke, with light and pleasureful guidance.

JOHANN WOLFGANG VON GOETHE

CAPRICORN
December 22 - January 19

The most conservative of all in the Zodiac is Capricorn, an Earth Sign, whose symbol is the Goat. He is ambitious, detailed, strong-willed and is always striving for something higher. Like the goat he climbs sure-footedly, constantly seeking for perfection. Conscientious and exacting, he takes pride in all that he does. Ready, will-

48

ing, and able to organize and arrange, he does this on a practical and efficient basis.

Capricorn has an urge to be of service and is interested in charitable group work.

Tactful and diplomatic, he finds the good will of the public essential to him. Personal prestige and worldly position are important. His desire to be well thought of makes him less inclined to go against convention than any other of the twelve signs. Though critical himself, he does not welcome criticism, even though it may be constructive and well meant.

Capricorn is admired and respected, has great loyalty to his family, but his natural reserve prevents him from making close friends easily. This cautiousness manifests itself in much of his thinking.

Capricorn is the businessman's sign. With steady work and the desire to get to the top, Capricorn often becomes the head of the company. His is also the scholarly sign producing teachers and philosophers.

CAUTION is the eldest child of wisdom.

VICTOR HUGO

THANK God every morning when you get up that you have something to do that day which must be done, whether you like it or not. Being forced to work and forced to do your best will breed in you temperance and self-control, diligence and strength of will, cheerfulness and content, and a hundred virtues which the idle never know.

CHARLES KINGSLEY

WHATEVER I have tried to do in this life, I have tried with all my heart to do well; whatever I have devoted myself to I have devoted myself to completely; in great aims and in small, I have always been thoroughly in earnest.

CHARLES DICKENS

IT is much easier to be critical than to be correct.

BENJAMIN DISRAELI

MEASURE not dispatch by the times of sitting, but by the advancement of the business.

FRANCIS BACON

PRIDE is as loud a beggar as want, and a great deal more saucy. When you have bought one fine thing, you must buy ten more, that your appearance may be all of a piece; but it is easier to suppress the first desire than to satisfy all that follow it.

BENJAMIN FRANKLIN

THE modesty of certain ambitious persons consists in becoming great without making too much noise; it may be said that they advance in the world on tiptoe.

VOLTAIRE

IT is much more important to be human than it is to be important.

THOMAS JEFFERSON

AN investment in knowledge always pays the best interest.

BENJAMIN FRANKLIN

NOTHING is more noble, nothing more venerable than fidelity. Faithfulness and truth are the most sacred excellences and endowments of the human mind.

CICERO

FEW things are impossible to diligence and skill.

SAMUEL JOHNSON

THERE is no man, no woman, so small but that they cannot make their life great by high endeavor.

THOMAS CARLYLE

THEN welcome each rebuff
That turns earth's smoothness rough,
Each sting that bids not sit nor stand,
    but go!
Be our joys three-parts pain!
Strive, and hold cheap the strain;
Learn, nor account the pang; dare, never
    grudge the throe!

ROBERT BROWNING

WE live by admiration, hope, and love.

WILLIAM WORDSWORTH

THOSE who educate children well are more to be honored than they who produce them; for these only gave them life, those the art of living well.

ARISTOTLE

AQUARIUS
January 20 - February 18

The symbol of Aquarius is the Water Bearer and the Element is that of Air, the Sign of the intellectual. 82% of the people in the American Hall of Fame are reputed to be Aquarians. This is the sign of human brotherhood, tolerance, and a sense of responsibility to the world. The Aquarian is unselfish, and truth is his goal.

53

An Aquarian does not work by the clock. He has dogged persistence, a fixity of purpose, and an inventive ability, second only to Gemini. His ideas are apt to differ so much from the average person that he may be classed as a "lone wolf." The petty concerns that disturb others do not seem to touch him. Highly intelligent and capable of analytical thinking, he may discard the classroom for practical experience. It is essential that the Aquarian discipline his mental activities.

Though he is social and deeply concerned with his fellow man, he is not especially interested in the individual. His sympathy is impersonal. Detached, he does not make many warm friendships but maintains a loyal relationship with family and intimates. He is not inclined to the marriage state, but once wedded, he seeks to maintain harmony. Quick of temper, he does not bear malice.

The gifted Aquarian does well in work where he can use his imagination and inventiveness. Routine work tires him. In social work and as a political figure, he finds great satisfaction. In writing he is able to express his humanitarian ideals.

BENEVOLENCE is one of the distinguishing characters of man. It is the path of duty.

MENCIUS

THE duty of man is plain and simple, and consists of but two points: his duty to God, which every man must feel; and his duty to his neighbor — to do as he would be done by.

THOMAS PAINE

THE greatest remedy for anger is delay.

SENECA

THE sweetest lives are those to duty wed,
Whose deeds, both great and small,
Are close knit strands of an unbroken
thread
Where love ennobles all.

. . . . . .

Thou shalt be served thyself by every sense
Of service which thou renderest.

ELIZABETH BARRETT BROWNING

55

INVENTION is activity of mind, as fire is air in motion; sharpening of the spiritual sight, to discern hidden aptitudes.

MARTIN FARQUHAR TUPPER

THE primal duties shine aloft, like stars;
The charities that soothe and heal and
    bless
Are scattered at the feet of men like
    flowers.

WILLIAM WORDSWORTH

THE race of mankind would perish from the earth did they cease to aid each other.

SIR WALTER SCOTT

THE responsibility of tolerance lies with those who have the wider vision.

GEORGE ELIOT

THE nurse of full-grown souls is solitude.

JAMES RUSSELL LOWELL

THE men who succeed best in public life are those who take the risk of standing by their own convictions.

JAMES ABRAM GARFIELD

IF a man does not keep pace with his companions, perhaps it is because he hears a different drummer. Let him step to the music he hears, however measured or far away.

HENRY DAVID THOREAU

THE great instrument of moral good is the imagination.

PERCY BYSSHE SHELLEY

RESPONSIBILITY walks hand in hand with capacity and power.

JOSIAH GILBERT HOLLAND

WHEN good men die, their goodness does
    not perish,
But lives though they are gone. As for
    the bad,
All that was theirs dies, and is buried with
    them.

EURIPIDES

THOSE who are quite satisfied, sit still and do nothing; those who are not quite satisfied, are the sole benefactors of the world.

WALTER SAVAGE LANDOR

PISCES
February 19 - March 20

Pisces has an unusual dual personality.
His symbol is that of two fish bound to-
gether — one swimming upstream against
the current and the other swimming in the
opposite direction with the tide. It is im-
portant that Pisces take a definite point of
view, for of all the signs in the Zodiac he
is the most receptive to outside influences.
The "still, small voice" reaches him direct-

ly, and every person, every situation makes an impression upon him. He is sensitive and has great psychic ability as do others under the Water Sign. He has tremendous empathy and knows how each individual feels.

Pisces likes people, enjoys being involved with them, and can adjust readily to various moods and temperaments. He has the capability of deep emotional attachments. He gives his complete affection and hopes to be loved devotedly in return; this may tend to make him jealous. As a rule, he may seem to be unemotional on the surface, but he is still water that runs deep.

Pisces requires companionship to fulfill his life. Children and animals are a special delight to him and they return the feeling double-fold. His kindness and generosity know no bounds.

Pisces, idealistic and philosophical, holds ideas on religion too firmly founded and too personal to be discussed, though on most subjects he is voluble. Sometimes a dreamer, he is industrious and methodi-

cal and a perfectionist where work is required.

Pisces has a great appreciation of the arts and often has talent in some creative field. He can find success in social work, religion, or as an executive in the field of his choice.

IN still waters are the largest fish.

DANISH PROVERB

GENEROSITY goes with good faith.

PIERRE CORNEILLE

PARENT of golden dreams, Romance!

LORD BYRON

IT is recorded of many great men, who did not end their days in a work house, that they were non-retentive of money. Schiller, when he had nothing else to give away, gave the clothes from his back, and Goldsmith the blankets from his bed. Tender hands found it necessary to pick Beethoven's pockets at home before he walked out.

EDWARD ROBERT BULWER-LYTTON

NEXT to love, sympathy is the divinest passion of the human heart.

EDMUND BURKE

I WOULD help others, out of a fellow-feeling.

ROBERT BURTON

QUICK sensitiveness is inseparable from a ready understanding.

JOSEPH ADDISON

A MOMENT'S insight is sometimes worth a life's experience.

OLIVER WENDELL HOLMES

YOU can see farther into a millstone than he.

MIGUEL DE CERVANTES

MY eyes make pictures when they are shut.

SAMUEL TAYLOR COLERIDGE

GIVE a little love to a child, and you get a great deal back.

JOHN RUSKIN

IN nature, as in seas, depth answers unto depth.

CHARLES DICKENS

CHILD of the pure, unclouded brow
    And dreaming eyes of wonder!
Though time be fleet and I and thou
    Are half a life asunder,
Thy loving smile will surely hail
The love-gift of a fairy-tale.

LEWIS CARROLL

OUR ideals are our better selves.

A. BRONSON ALCOTT

JEALOUSY'S eyes are green.

PERCY BYSSHE SHELLEY

SMOOTH runs the water where the brook is deep.

PROVERB

THE more a man loves, the more he suffers. The sum of possible grief for each soul is in proportion to its degree of perfection.

HENRI-FRÉDÉRIC AMIEL